Quests

Travel Stories of
Seeking and Finding

Jan Alkire

Byron Books
Box 51072
Seattle, WA 98115-1072

Website: www.JanAlkire.com

ISBN: 0-9679815-2-2

Library of Congress Control Number: 2013921542

Cover design by Ray Meuse
Cover photograph by Fred Alkire
Printed and bound by Gorham Printing, Centralia, Washington

"Quest" © 1988; used by permission of the
Elizabeth B. Rooney Family Trust
Contact information at www.brighamfarm.com

Photo at Children's Orthopedic Hospital published Friday,
February 10, 1967. © 1967, Seattle Times Company.
Used with permission.

*To my family, with love: Fred, Beth, Kathy,
grandchildren, sisters, brothers, nieces, nephews, and
all "outlaws" (i.e., in-laws). Each of you has touched
my life and blessed me in countless ways.*

*And to those family members who went before me:
Parents, grandparents and, especially, those
earlier ancestors who had the courage to leave their
homeland and come to the United States.*

CONTENTS

PREFACE

Leap the tall hedges
That enclose your mind
And ride your winged dreams
Into the far, far reaches of the sky.

Leave far behind
The small things you were sure of.
Go and find
The "things in heaven and earth"
Which this old world
Has not imagined yet.

Go
And do not forget
To bring back moons and miracles
So we who stay at home
Can also start to see.[1]

1   "Quest" by Elizabeth Brigham Rooney from *All Miracle*. Used with permission.

Long before I read this poem by my father's cousin Elizabeth, I longed to "leap the tall hedges" of my mind and my life. I wanted to ride winged dreams to places known to others, but not to me. So in 1965, I left far behind the things I was sure of and sailed off to see the world.

Part of my quest was clear: meet the descendants of my German great-grandparents. Other goals looked more like fuzzy photographs. I sought without knowing what I was seeking, looked without knowing what I would find.

An attitude of seeking opened my mind to find more than I expected. It toppled my young-adult illusions of self-mastery, especially when looking for—and failing to find—a road, a meal, a bathroom, a bed. Most of all, seeking filled my days and nights with surprises, many of them joyful, some of them painful. I returned home a different person than who I was when I left.

In her poem, Elizabeth Rooney urges us to "bring back moons and miracles so we who stay at home can also start to see." That is why I have written this book.

Part One

Europe

My cousin Ingemi, ca. age 12

Chapter 1:
Seeking "A Grand Adventure"

"Whatever you can do, or dream you can, begin it.
Boldness has genius, power, and magic in it."

Goethe

A ship in the middle of a hurricane is no fun at all. You rock and roll—without the music. A dinner that's set before you may slide over and end up in front of the person next to you. You fall to the floor if you let go of a fixed object. And if you're like me, one of the fortunate few who doesn't get seasick, you're lonely because most other passengers are busy being sick in their stateroom. It's just you, the crew, and that screaming, howling, never-ending wind.

This hurricane struck in the Atlantic Ocean on Day 4 of a trip I took to Europe in 1965. Remove a century and my sailing would resemble an opposite crossing taken by my great-grandparents in 1865. That's when Carl Karstens and his fiancé, Wilhelmina Scheibel, came to America in one of the world's first steamers. Erase the limits of time, and our ships could have passed each other in the night, each carrying us with our dreams and reasons for going where we were going.

Wilhelmina (better known as Minna) had three brothers in Madison, Wisconsin. Was that the only reason she and Carl came here from Germany? What had life been like where they lived? Why did Minna's sister, Sophie, remain behind? No one today knows.

However, their decision to emigrate to the United States surely changed Carl and Minna's lives in profound ways, especially since they never returned to their homeland.

My reasons for going to Europe were light-hearted and vague: I was in my mid-20s and in search of a "grand adventure". What I found transformed my view of the world, my awareness of America and, ultimately, my entire future.

In the beginning...

1951. Looking back now, I think my adventures in 1965 actually began fourteen years earlier when I was recovering from a childhood illness-of-the-month—I think it was mumps. As I lay in bed one afternoon staring at the pattern of cracks on the ceiling, Mom brought me a letter from my grandmother, Nanna.[2] She wrote that I had a cousin my age living in Germany who wanted to become pen pals. Would I like that? Hm-m-m. Cousin; foreign country; pen pals. That sounded like fun. And so, with no TV in our house and nothing better to do that day than stare at those ceiling cracks, I got out a pencil and paper and wrote to my cousin. Her name, Nanna said, was Ingemi.

Thus began the expansion of my mind. First came a shock: I learned that Ingemi's and my mail would be inspected by secret police. What? *Why?* Because Ingemi and her mother, Margot, were living in Communist-controlled East Germany. Any East German who said negative things about Communism got in trouble. And if the police didn't like a piece of incoming mail, it never reached its destination.

Because of this fear of censorship, Ingemi and I had a rather stilted correspondence, and I had no idea how bleak and scary her life in East Germany was. Most terrifying for her and her mother: families vanishing in the middle of the night. Had the secret police seized

---

2   Nanna was one of Carl and Minna's four children.

them, or had they escaped to freedom? No one knew; everyone lived in fear. Many families decided they couldn't endure this oppression, so they risked their lives to escape to West Germany. They wanted a whole lot more than adventure. They dreamed of freedom.[3]

Freedom

1961. Fast forward ten years. I was a junior at the University of Wisconsin, dissecting cadavers in an anatomy class, then later coping with the smell of formaldehyde that clung to my hands like Styrofoam beads. Worse yet: memorizing the Latin-sounding name for parts in the human body. Taking a mail break one day from my efforts to cram more words into my brain, I was amazed to receive a postcard from Ingemi saying, "We're free!" Wow! She and Margot had escaped from East Germany through West Berlin. However, freedom for them had come at a heavy price: They had left house, clothes, books, family treasures, and everything else they owned except a black Newfoundland named Tesse. Could I do that today?—leave everything and start over with nothing? It would take a whole lot of suffering and a whole lot of courage before I'd be willing to do what they did.

Freedom meant that Ingemi and I now could say what we wanted to say in our letters. We got to know each other better until, after awhile, I decided that if I could save enough money, I would travel to Europe to meet her and her mother. I wanted to "see the world" and, along the way, meet Ingemi and Margot.

My decision became such a focal point for me that I even gave up a serious dating relationship and marriage proposal in order to achieve it. I knew I was too restless for marriage and would make a lousy wife until I got rid of my wandering itch. So there I was at the

---

3   For a brief look at Germany's situation in the aftermath of World War II, see the appendix.

dream phase of my grand adventure, already making a decision that would have an impact on the rest of my life.

"Ride your winged dreams into the far, far reaches of the sky."

1963. Graduation day was nearing when I would receive a degree in physical therapy. Adulthood—yeah! But then what? Classmates around me were talking about china and silver patterns for upcoming weddings. Me? I didn't even know where I wanted to live. Based on what one of our professors told us, options were limitless: "Close your eyes, put your finger down on a map of the United States," she said, "and you can get a job there as a PT." Nice. Very nice. But in a way, this infinity of choices made me anxious, like a toddler who gets whiny when offered ten options for breakfast rather than, perhaps, just two.

Decisions, decisions.... First on my mental list came the East Coast. I crossed off Washington DC because women there outnumbered men by a huge percentage. Boston? I eliminated it because at that time the Boston Strangler was busy killing single women in the medical field. New York City? Too crowded. How about the West Coast?

Through a thought process that perhaps only a young adult can understand, I eventually chose to live in Seattle. I knew nothing about it, but that didn't matter. Clueless about life's potential pitfalls, I simply packed two suitcases, hopped on a train in Chicago with $50 in my pocket, and hopped off when the train reached the end of the line. My father thought I would return home so fast that I shouldn't even take a suitcase with me. Ha! I've lived here ever since.

My college professor was right: I found a good job within two days, then settled into a life of building friendships, dating, and experiencing the joys of life without school. Along with that fun, however, the dream of travel remained, and I began planning for my trip. I can summarize those plans in two words: scrimp and save. Two years later, I had enough money to go to Europe with a friend named Libby who, like me, wanted to see life beyond America.[4] We decided to discover it together. Little did we know all that awaited us beyond this continent.

Thoughts:

"All journeys have secret destinations of
which the traveler is unaware."

Martin Buber

---

4   One thing helped make this trip possible: a strong dollar in the 1960s that meant Americans could travel in Europe cheaply. (A best-seller those days was titled *Europe on $5 a Day*—and you really could get by on that amount.)

Schnapsy traveled in all kinds of weather!

Chapter 2:
Finding Adventures
—and Kindness

"Leave far behind the small things you were sure of".
In September 1965 Libby and I boarded a ship in New York City and set out on our big adventure. Our first "adventure" was that hurricane in the Atlantic Ocean. What waves! What wind! And, for Libby, what seasickness! But the ship finally made it to Germany. We stepped on dry land with shaky knees and an odd sensation that the ground beneath our feet was moving—a feeling that lasted for several days.

At the dock a bright red VW Beetle was waiting for me, gleaming in the sun. With my parents' help, I had gotten a loan for it back in the States and now here it was, my first car. I gave her a German name—Schnapsy ("little brandy")—because she was, after all, a German car. I immediately bonded with Schnapsy as if she were my pal, my soulmate, my automotive buddy. What a thrill.

More thrills appeared as soon as we left the docks because traffic signs in Europe were in symbols instead of the words Libby and I understood back home. The symbols looked like hieroglyphics to us, so this made our first few days of driving in Europe quite exciting— the kind of excitement you feel when you think you might die in the next minute or two. We drove the wrong way down one-way streets. We drove on sidewalks. We parked in no-parking zones. Once I even drove Schnapsy up over a curb and onto the grass in the middle of a traffic circle. Bewildered, we sat there for a minute wondering what had happened while drivers going around the circle stared at us.

The two of us soon figured out how to read road signs. We did this while doing a "sweeping tour" through many countries in 30 days. We went from Norway down to Spain and Portugal, then back north again. Along the way, we stopped and met Ingemi and Margot (described later in Chapter 4). But mostly we drove and drove and drove—a different town or even a different country each day. Several mornings I had a brief feeling of panic when I woke up: Where am I? What country am I in?

We used guidebooks to learn how to say a few words in each language. At the very least we wanted to be able to say "please", "thank you", "hello", and "goodbye". Our guidebooks also included short sentences that tourists might need in their travels. One sentence in the books made us laugh because it felt so out of place for a tourist: "Will you marry me?" ("Hello. Where is a restaurant? Will you marry me?")

I had met foreigners in the United States. Now Libby and I were the foreigners. We were the ones who didn't know the languages that natives knew, the ones who needed to learn new customs. And we were the ones who often got amazingly, strikingly lost.

"We've gotten to know people mostly through the fantastic predicaments we've found ourselves in—for instance, the reindeer hunters on top of a Norwegian fjord. We ended up singing German beer-drinking songs with them—rifles nearby and a howling gale in our ears." [5]

I have fond memories of Libby's and my "grand tour" through Europe. The two of us met many wonderful people. Along the way I learned a lot about kindness and what a life-saver it can be for the hapless stranger who is wandering around lost, hungry, and in need.

---

5   This, along with other italicized quotes within the text, are from letters I wrote home during my trip.

I still feel grateful for all the kindness shown towards the two of us when we were foreigners.

Thoughts:

"One kind word can warm three winter months."

Japanese proverb

Chapter 3:
Pursuing New Languages;
Discovering Many Cultures

"All I know is that I know nothing."

Socrates

Language barriers

Libby and I tried to say foreign words correctly, and usually people understood us. Occasionally they didn't. For instance, a guidebook told us the way to say "thank you" in Norwegian was "tak". So when someone in Norway would do something for us, we would smile and say, "tak." They would look at us strangely. Eventually we were befriended by a Norwegian who was fluent in English. We asked why people were looking at us strangely whenever we said, "thank you".

"How are you saying it?" he asked.

"Tak," we answered. He looked at us strangely.

"I hate to tell you this," he said, "but you've been going through Norway saying 'top of the roof' to everyone." He tried to teach us how to say "tak" correctly, but our ears couldn't hear the difference between his "tak" and our "tak".

We met many Europeans who knew English. When we had a need, usually someone could help us. They helped us find hotels, bathrooms, restaurants, and much more. They showed us how to get from "a" to "z" and all points in between.

Occasionally no one could speak English. I remember a small restaurant where the menu was in Norwegian and no one could tell us what the items were. So we picked a price, pointed to the menu, then waited to see what we'd be having for dinner. When the server brought our food, everyone in the room stopped talking and looked at us. They knew we had no idea what we had ordered. The server put the plates in front of us and we laughed when we saw it was hash. Thank heavens we hadn't pointed to something like stinky cheese.

One day a language barrier became a crisis. We were in Spain and had found lodging at a former convent that now was a low-cost historic inn for tourists. I was standing at the open window in our room, looking out onto a garden filled with flowers. A woman sang in the garden as the sun was setting. Such peace. Such beauty.

But then, such a crisis. I turned on a lamp in the room and electrical sparks came shooting out from the wall socket. Help! Libby was out. I was alone. What should I do? I rocketed out of the room, ran down the hall, found the manager, and yelled, "Fire!" He looked at me blankly. "No comprendo," he said.

Memories of high school Spanish told me the man was saying, "I don't understand." *No, no,* I thought. *This is no time for a language barrier. Maybe he'll understand if I speak more slowly.* So I leaned closer and said, "Fi-i-r-r-e!" He just shrugged and said, "No comprendo."

Time for show-and-tell. Using gestures, I got the manager to follow me to our room. I ran; he walked. When we arrived, sparks were still shooting out from the wall socket. "Ah," he said, "*Fuego.*"

"Fuego..., fuego," I muttered, touching a finger to my forehead. "Never forget this word, Jan. *Fuego.*" While I was memorizing this vocabulary word, the manager was strolling over to the wall outlet. I could see that he was about to unplug the lamp. "No, no!" I yelled. I imagined electrocution, not knowing that because this inn used DC current, the outlet wasn't dangerous. The manager unplugged the lamp; no more *fuego*. He shrugged his shoulders (again) and left the room, saying, "Americana" (meaning me).

I wanted to say, "Sir, if you ever come to America, do not do what you just did. It will drop you in your tracks. It will fry you like an egg. Your hair will stand on end. You will die." But he would not have understood any of that because we had a language barrier. Too bad.

Learning a foreign language

Language barriers must have been an issue for my great-grandparents when they arrived in the U.S. in 1865. Eventually Carl learned to speak English, but Minna never did—this in spite of the fact that she lived in America for the rest of her life: 41 years in all. A problem? Perhaps not a huge one because in the 1800s, areas of many cities were split into different nationalities: Chinatown, Germantown, Little Italy, Little Poland, Little Whatever. Every nationality had its own language, its own churches, its own stores, its own doctors, its own life. Most large cities contained mini-cities of immigrants.

Libby and I were planning to stay in Germany for awhile and didn't want to be a two-person Little America. So after our tour through many countries, we drove to Lüneburg, outside of Hamburg. There we began classes at a foreign language school called the Goethe Institut.

*"The Institut is the best cross-section of the world I think
I'll ever encounter. From Iceland to Hong Kong to Nigeria to Peru to
Norway to Afghanistan—we all bring our own cultures together under
the same roof and strive for a common goal: learn German.
We could start a miniature United Nations here."*

Learning a foreign language was an adventure for Libby and me. For other students, it was serious business. For instance, two American opera singers were there to improve their ability to sing German operas. A Mormon young man planned to do mission work in West Berlin. Several men from the Middle East hoped to become doctors, but their country had no medical school. Before attending a German school, they had to learn the language. Each student had a dream; the dreams met in that small town in West Germany.

Classes took place six days a week. All teaching was done in German. Every day for two months, it was German. Morning, noon, and night: German. Each of us lived with a host family and spoke German. When we went to buy something in a store, we spoke German. (And if we didn't ask for the item using *correct* grammar, we didn't receive it.)

"What's new in my life these days? New words, for one thing—over 1,000 of them in three weeks. My poor feeble brain is spinning."

By the end of each day, my brain felt tired. It felt like I had been doing math all day. I would have a thought in English, then translate it into German. Then I would speak the thought to someone. That person would answer me in German. Then inside my head I would translate what they said into English. On and on it went. What a lot of mental work!

"We bring our own cultures together under the same roof ..."

All of us learned more than German at the Institut. We got to know each other, including our nationalities and cultures. For instance, in our classroom Libby sat next to an 18-year-old Saudi student. One day Libby turned and asked him what time it was. He blushed, got all flustered, and could hardly stammer out an answer. Later Libby asked an older Saudi student if she had been rude to her classmate. "You didn't do anything wrong," he said. "You're just the first woman he has ever spoken to other than his mother and his sister."

Meanwhile, back home...

At the time I left for Europe, I was dating two men: Bob and Fred. I saw my relationship with Bob as one that might lead to marriage. Fred seemed like a more casual date—a great guy, yes, but until the gift of distance came between these two men and me, Bob was at the forefront of my mind.

I wrote to Bob and Fred, and they wrote to me. But what a difference in their letters! Bob's were infrequent, and when he did write, I often had to ask Libby what he was talking about. One letter said he'd been a subject in a government study on the effects of LSD. After that, his messages became increasingly scattered, and I was dismayed when he wrote me once from San Francisco's Haight Ashbury district (a center of the drug culture in the '60s). I kept on writing to him, but at the back of my mind was a question: Who is this guy, anyway?

Meanwhile, Fred's letters were revealing, funny, newsy, and deep. He sounded grounded, not spaced out on a hallucinogenic drug. Then came the day at the Goethe Institut when a postman came into our classroom and handed me a package. The moment class ended, I opened the package and saw... a photo album, dedicated to me and filled with pictures Fred had taken and developed himself—photos of Mt. Rainier, Mt. Adams, Puget Sound, the Space Needle. Also photos of strangers and photos of me. Everyone in class ooh-ed and aah-ed at what they were seeing. What a treasure.

"There seems to be a general consensus now that the U.S. is indeed a grand country—not only filled with cowboys, gangsters, and Hollywood stars, but also blessed with some of the most awesome natural beauty in the world."

While my classmates poured over the photos, a seismic shift was taking place in my mind. Fred was looking like a *really* great guy—including incredibly thoughtful. Hm-m-m.

Thoughts:

"Act as if what you do makes a difference. It does."

William James

Germany in the 1960s, showing places I visited.

Chapter 4:
Facing Communism;
Finding Gratitude for Freedom

"Democracy is the worst form of government except for all those other forms that have been tried from time to time."

Winston Churchill

After two months of German classes, Libby and I could speak and read enough German to get along. Where would we go now? My host family at the Goethe Institut said they knew a hotel owner in West Berlin who was looking for maids to do extra work before the holidays. If we would work four hours a day, she would give us free lodging and meals.

We liked this idea. It would give us a place to stay and make our American dollars last longer. From 8:00 a.m. to noon, each of us would be a "putzfrau"—a cleaning lady. Then for the rest of the day we could go out, be tourists, and meet people. We also would be able to see what life was like in a free city in the middle of a Communist country: East Germany.[6]

A Communist border

Driving to West Berlin meant dealing with Communist borders and Communist guards. Neither of us knew exactly how hard it would be when we set out in Schnapsy on a snowy December morning.

As we arrived at the border between East and West Germany, the

---

6   At the time of our visit, West Germany and West Berlin were democratic; East Germany was Communist; West Berlin existed in democratic isolation inside East Germany. See the appendix for more background.

first person we met was a huge Russian guard with a machine gun. He walked slowly towards us with the gun pointed at my head. He was frowning. In fact, he looked as if he had not smiled in years. He looked as if a smile might make his face crack.

This guard could have won a scaring-people contest. I started to panic. What should I do? Perhaps my passport would keep me safe, but where was it?

"Libby, quick!" I said. "I need my passport. Where is it?"

"Jan," said Libby. "You're holding it in your hand."

"Oh. Oh yes."

The guard took away our passports, which made me feel as if I'd suddenly lost all my human rights.

"When you're in the hands of unfriendly authorities in a foreign country, an American passport feels like a security blanket— a combined Declaration of Independence, American Constitution and American flag all rolled up in one. Having it taken away by an armed guard is a crisis."

After surrendering our passports, we were told to unload everything from our car. "Everything" was a lot. Out came four large suitcases into the snow, plus other smaller ones; out came ski boots, climbing boots, sleeping bags, a guitar (mine), a typewriter (Libby's), and cartons of books.

Eventually my once-filled VW was empty, and guards started going through all our stuff. Away went some of our books, including a Bible and a philosophy book. I knew religion had been suppressed in Communist countries, so the loss of the Bible didn't surprise me. But why confiscate a philosophy book? That was weird.

While some guards searched our belongings, others searched the VW. They measured the inside, then the outside. What in the world??... Later I learned they wanted to make sure we hadn't built a tiny hiding place inside the car—space for some escapee we might pick up in East Germany. Meanwhile, another guard ran a mirror under the car to see if someone was strapped to the bottom. Then he put a measuring stick into the gas tank to see if we had a tiny false tank and a large hidden space where the gas tank should be.

All this searching took place while we stood like statues in the snow. I wondered if we would be allowed to drive through East Germany in order to get to West Berlin. I wondered if we would get our passports back. I wondered what kind of madness this was.

West Berlin

Finally the guards gave our passports back to us and told us to go. We drove into East Germany, a barren, polluted land. We drove until we reached the border between East Germany and West Berlin. Away went our passports. Out came everything from the VW. This time, however, the cartoon of books elicited a different response than the one we'd had at the earlier border:

> "It was the books which got the Communist inspector—
> he was as excited as a schoolboy with a new toy and sat in
> the backseat of Schnapsy for an interminable time,
> reading avidly, laughing, and excitedly asking questions while
> we stood outside the car in the snow and wind."

Thanks be to God, the inspector eventually finished his library reading and everyone else finished searching, measuring and hunting for escapees. They returned our passports and allowed us to enter West Berlin.

What a difference West Berlin was from the country surrounding it. One minute it felt like we were in a black-and-white movie. The next minute the movie turned to color. I felt like Dorothy coming into the Land of Oz. West Berlin was filled with bright lights, bright colors, and new buildings. It radiated energy.

"If Berlin were a person she would be sitting on the edge of her chair. And well she might, for the situation here is probably unequaled in history."

We drove through crowded streets until we found the hotel where we would work and live for the next few weeks. We soon learned that the owner wanted her hotel to be *very* clean. We vacuumed, scoured, swept, and polished. We got down on our hands and knees and scrubbed tiled bathroom floors with little brushes. The landlady also gave us shovels and told us to get rid of the pigeon poop on the balconies. As we shoveled, Libby said, "People at home aren't going to believe me when I tell them some of the things I did in Europe."

Our time in West Berlin wasn't all work. On the ship coming to Europe, we had met a West Berlin architect named Horst. He showed us lovely places in his city, taught us about architecture, invited us to parties. Everywhere we went, I tried to speak German because it helped me get to know German people and their customs. Plus, I enjoyed the challenge of a new language.

Horst also took us to concerts and theaters. One particular performance remains etched in my mind: a German translation of Shakespeare's *Taming of the Shrew*. I understood a total of three words: "Küss mich, Käthe"—"Kiss me, Kate". (Shakespeare? in *German*? What was I thinking when I accepted that invitation?)

East Berlin

One day Horst volunteered to give us a tour of East Berlin. Saying yes meant dealing with a near-impregnable barrier between freedom and Communism: the Berlin Wall. To get beyond the Wall, we had to go through "Checkpoint Charlie". Guards, searches, machine guns, the temporary loss of passports: We were getting used to this.

Finally the three of us got through Checkpoint Charlie and drove into East Berlin. The first thing I noticed? No cars. A city of over one million people had only one traffic light that worked. Even that light didn't seem to be needed. West Berlin was packed with cars and traffic lights and traffic jams. East Berlin looked empty.

The second thing I noticed about the city? A number of buildings still lay in ruins created by World War II bombings. Twenty years after the war, parts of East Berlin looked as though those bombs had been dropped last week. The area looked totally different from West Berlin, which had been rebuilt.

The third thing I noticed about East Berlin? Everything looked gray. Gray people wearing gray clothes walked next to gray buildings. They were almost pressed up against the buildings, as if those walls could keep them safe. No one smiled. No one looked happy. No one looked free.

Horst's tour was what I call our "real" visit to East Berlin. Earlier, Libby and I had taken an official bus tour that covered only a few restored avenues and highlighted several restored buildings. It was led by a young man about our age.

"The guide talked to me for about 20 minutes about East Germany, Communism, and his work. In the interest of physical safety and of acquiring more information, I just sat and listened—listened in amazement to words that were said in all seriousness but which were twisted to the point of absurdity. It was all I could do to keep a blank face, especially to statements like the one that people behind the Iron Curtain can't travel out of its boundaries because the West won't let them!"

Under attack

I liked the energy and beauty of West Berlin. I liked the people. What I didn't like was being surrounded by a totalitarian state. It pained me to hear gunfire at night, gunfire that was coming from the Berlin Wall as people tried to escape. I felt very sad for them and, yes, anxious for my own safety. The gunfire gave me auditory proof of the city's fragility.

My fear became highly focused one night when Libby and I awoke to the sound of cannons going off, followed by a barrage of machine gun fire. I sat bolt upright in bed. "Of all the rotten luck!" I said. "We're here for less than a month and *this* is when East Germany decides to invade the city. What are we going to do?"

Libby, ever the humorist in a crisis situation, said, "I don't know about you, Jan, but right now I'm already wearing 2 pairs of pants, 4 pairs of underpants, and 3 shirts." Ha, ha. Libby was ready to make her escape without any luggage.

We sat listening to the artillery, expecting everyone in the hotel to be rushing around, slamming doors, running. But no. Nobody stirred. After about 15 minutes on high alert, we decided this must be some "quaint custom" that we didn't understand, so we went to back to sleep. However I had to work at staying asleep because outside it sounded like an ongoing performance of the end of Tchaikovsky's 1812 Overture—lots of booming and crashing, but minus the music.

The next morning we arrived at breakfast bleary-eyed and in search of an explanation for the previous night's drama. "What was that?" we asked the landlady. "Those were war maneuvers," she said. "Sometimes the military forces here pretend we're being invaded." Oh. Well, in Libby's and my case, they succeeded. It sounded real to us.

Before and after...

Libby and I left West Berlin after three weeks. If someone had told me the Wall would be torn down in 1989, I wouldn't have believed it. Communism looked powerful enough to last forever. Yet twenty-four years after we were there, East and West Germany were reunited because Communism in Eastern Europe had collapsed and, along with it, the Berlin Wall. Totalitarianism had lost. Freedom had won.

Before Berlin, freedom for me had simply been part of American history, a Liberty Bell in Philadelphia, a concept I studied in school. It had surrounded me like the air I breathed, so invisible that I barely recognized its existence. After Berlin, freedom became almost sensory—something I could feel, taste, see, hear. It became precious to me because I knew I could lose it. I've never taken it for granted since then.

War and Peace

1865-1965. It had been 100 years since Wilhelminna Scheibel said goodbye to her sister Sophie and sailed to America with her fiancé. A lot had happened between the United States and Germany during the 20th century. Our nations were friends now but had only recently been enemies.

Nanna had told me that Ingemi's father, Bahne, died in a Nazi concentration camp because of his opposition to Hitler. That's not what happened. Margot said that because he was a large-animal veterinarian – a vital profession at home – he was able to avoid fighting in World War II until Hitler invaded Russia. Then he was drafted and sent to the Eastern Front. Like so many other soldiers who fought and died in that arena, he never was heard from again. After World War II, there was great hunger and suffering in Germany. Nanna and her brother, Frank, heard about this and sent food, clothing, and medical funds to Margot and Ingemi. The two of them told us they would always be grateful to their American relatives for helping them when they were in need. Our countries had gone to war, but our family had stayed together.

Chapter 5:
Seeking and
Finding Family Ties

"Call it a clan, call it a network, call it a tribe, call it a family.
Whatever you call it, whoever you are, you need one."

Jane Howard, writer

Now let us turn back the clock to when Libby and I first arrived in
Europe. When we were doing our "grand tour"of many countries, one
of our top desires was to visit Ingemi and Margot. So we made sure
our route included their home in the Black Forest in the southern
part of West Germany.

Seeking my relatives

Margot's home was in the mountains in a village called Schweikof.
On a sunny September day we drove Schnapsy up a narrow road until
a sign told us we had arrived. But where were the houses? All we saw
were a few barns. Where did the people live? We found out they lived
in those buildings. Half of each was for animals and the other half
was for people. For a city girl like me, this was a shock. I grew up in
suburbs of New York City and Chicago, where meat and milk came
from supermarkets, not animals. Now here I was in a different world,
a world where animals and people lived side by side.

Having found Schweikof, now we needed to find Margot and
Ingemi. Only 14 people lived there, so you would think it would be
hard to get lost, wouldn't you? Not so. We got lost. When we first
arrived, I had gone up to a woman and said "Margot". It looked like
she pointed to a dirt road that would lead to her home. That's not

where it took us. Instead, the "road" became narrower and narrower until we realized we had made a mistake. This was no road. This was a cow path. We couldn't turn back because the path had become very steep. We were in a pasture on a mountain side, and ahead of us was... a stream. Help!

Libby was driving; I was thinking of how to get us out of this mess. We had about five seconds to decide what to do because that water was getting closer and closer. Finally we both said, "When in doubt, keep moving." So that's what we did: drove straight into the stream. In we went on one side, out we came on the other. And there was the cow path again, only now we were driving up the side of the mountain instead of down.

Schnapsy chugged up the path until we reached a road that was actually a road. There, waiting for us, was the entire population of Schweikof, including Margot and Ingemi. Everyone had nervously watched us make our "big entrance." Now they were cheering. Margot came up and gave us hugs and said, "You're the first Americans to ever visit this village. These people think you're the 8th Wonder of the World."

Margot and Ingemi's home

After our dramatic arrival, Margot and Ingemi took us to their home, which was on the second floor of one of the buildings. There were three small rooms: a kitchen, a living room, and a bedroom. The bedroom was separated from the other two rooms by a hallway that led into the barn half of the building. The hallway also led to a second-floor latrine.

Homes in Schweikof did not have flush toilets and bathtubs and central heating and other comforts. This was fine with me because I saw it as part of our adventure. But would I want to use a latrine every day back home? No. Would I want to heat up water on a stove in order to take a bath? No. Would I want to bathe in a washtub set out in the middle of the kitchen? No. Experiences like these showed me what a good life I had in America. It gave me a sense of gratitude. It also led me to ask myself, "Have I been just a teeny bit spoiled?" Yes.

Time together

During this first visit, the four of us took walks in the Black Forest with their dog, Tesse. We talked, we laughed, we ate, we learned about each other's country and families. Then it was time for Libby and me to continue our tour of European countries. As we said goodbye, Margot invited us to return and spend Christmas with them. What a wonderful idea! We said yes. Then we drove down the mountain and headed south toward Spain and Portugal.

At Christmas we avoided all cow paths and went straight to Margot's home. Snow lay on the ground and it was *cold*. Back home, we might not have noticed this so much because our furnace-heated homes kept us cozy no matter how low the temperature got. But without central heating, cold crept in at night when the fire in heating stoves went out. I would wake up in the morning and see that the water in my water glass had frozen. So I would reach out, grab my clothes, and get dressed while I was still in bed.

One memory of this visit: cutting down a Christmas tree in the woods, setting it up in the living room, and decorating it with candles. When the candles were lit, we would sit back and gaze at its beauty. If a candle burned close to a branch, Ingemi would go over and pinch out the flame with her fingers. Her alertness didn't keep me from asking myself a question: "How many seconds would it take a flame to set fire to this tree and burn this place down?"

On Christmas Day we gave each other small gifts but the biggest gift was simply being together. Later that day, Libby and I went to Mass in a lovely Catholic church at the base of the mountain. We were in a foreign country thousands of miles from America; celebrating the birth of Christ in that church made me feel at home.

New Year's Eve in Giessen

After a wonderful Christmas week, Libby and I drove Ingemi to Giessen in the central part of West Germany in time for the start of her classes at the University of Giessen. There she introduced us to her fiancé, Claus, plus two friends and a dog named Jan. (A dog with the same name as mine? Weird. His was pronounced differently from mine—like "yan"—but still, it felt weird.) One thing about him: He didn't understand my commands such as "sit." He only understood them in German. "Wow," I said. "A dog who speaks German!" Then I laughed. Of course, dogs don't speak. They do, however, get trained to understand commands in one language. Instead of saying "sit" to Jan, I had to say, "Mach Platz."

So there we were: six young adults and one dog in a college town. It was New Year's Eve. What could we do but have a New Year's Eve party? We had German music and German beer and German food and German fun. We celebrated the end of 1965 and the start of 1966. Then Ingemi, Libby and I went back to Ingemi's apartment. Libby and I rolled out our sleeping bags on the floor of the living room. I was very tired.

One hour after we got to sleep, Libby's alarm went off. She sat up in her sleeping bag and said, "Happy New Year in London!" Then she lay back down.

"What are you doing?" I groaned.

"I'm wishing people a Happy New Year in every time zone," she said. Oh no.

Thank heavens for the time zones in the Atlantic Ocean. The alarm didn't go off for awhile. But then began the Time Zone March across America: "Happy New Year in New York! (home of my brother)." One hour later: "Happy New Year in Chicago!" (home of

Libby's parents and my parents). One hour later: "Happy New Year in Denver!" (someone's home—I forget whose.) And one hour later: "Happy New Year in Seattle!" (my home).

By now it was time to get up. I felt stiff from sleeping on the floor and dead tired from all the "happy new years". And did I mention a bit too much partying? The six of us gathered for brunch at Claus' apartment, and the only one who looked good was the dog.

During my visits with Ingemi, we became more than cousins. We also became friends. I liked her sense of humor. I saw her love and care for Margot, who often was nervous and anxious. Plus, I could see that Ingemi was serious about her studies. Her classes in veterinary medicine would start soon, so it was time for Libby and me to go. I still cherish memories of the days we had with Ingemi, Margot, Claus, and their friends. Many days, many hours, many blessings.

Thoughts:

"The best things in life aren't things."

Art Buchwald

"No Foreigners"

Not many apartments were available for rent in the mid -1960s because escapees from East Germany were coming into the area. They needed housing as much as we did. Result: a housing shortage.

Understandably, landlords put the needs of East Germans ahead of our needs. But we also noticed that many Germans looked down on foreign workers, who were called "guest workers". They did the manual labor others didn't want to do. Since the two of us were looking for an apartment, we must be guest workers, not tourists. Result: many closed doors.

Chapter 6:
Hunting for Housing and Jobs
—Any Housing, Any Jobs

"Don't be discouraged because you are discouraged."

St. Francis de Sales

From tourists to immigrants

After the holidays, Libby and I decided to look for work in Germany. We didn't know it then, but we were about to experience a big shift. We were going to cease being tourists (lots of fun) and students (lots of work but still a lot of fun). For awhile, we were going to be immigrants (lots of work and often not a lot of fun). So we packed our belongings into Schnapsy (again), said good-bye to Ingemi, and headed south to Munich in the Bavarian part of Germany.

Hunting for housing

Our first need in Munich: lodging. When Libby and I went to look at places, we would knock on a door and say we wanted to see the apartment that was listed for rent; the person who had answered would say, "No foreigners," and shut the door. Ouch.

While looking for a place to live, we stayed with a friend we had met earlier. But she lived with her parents, and their place was small. We knew we were crowding them. Plus, we could recall a quote from Benjamin Franklin: "Fish and visitors stink in three days."

It had been a lot longer than three days and we were getting desperate. Where could we go? The solution came from our other big task: job hunting.

My job hunt

As we looked for lodging in Munich, each of us also looked for a job. I wanted to work as a physical therapist, and there were openings in that field. Good. However, to work as a PT, I needed to be able to speak, read, and write German at a college level. Not good. I now spoke German at about a fifth-grade level. My reading and writing abilities were lower than that. This was going to keep me from working in my profession.

Job hunting brought me face-to-face with another problem: Before I could get a job, I had to have a work permit. But before I could get a work permit, I had to have a job. Around I went, from government offices to job prospects and back—a fine example of "Catch-22", but it didn't feel fine to me. It felt maddening.

What to do, what to do.... One day I remembered a letter of introduction an aunt had given me. She said if I ever needed a job in Munich, she knew a physician there. I needed a job in Munich, so would this be a good time to make use of my aunt's contact? Why not? I dug the letter out of my suitcase, found the physician's office, met him, and gave him the letter. Of course it said wonderful things about me. (It was, after all, written by my aunt.)

The man liked the letter and my PT credentials. He said he had a job opening for an aide. Would I accept that? Yes, I would. He hired me. Then he introduced me to an osteopath working for him, a young British woman named Rosemary.

More good news: Rosemary said she lived in an apartment that had a kitchen, a bathroom, and separate living areas for three people. One room was available. Did I need a place to live? Indeed I did. So in only a few hours I had found both a job and a place to live. Happy day for me! I thought it also was a happy day for Libby because she would be able to live with me for at least awhile.

Apartment living

My room had a bed, a dresser, a couple of chairs, a table, and a little heater that operated on oil. When I wanted heat, I put a few coins into a meter as if I were paying for parking. It was January; I wanted heat; I fed the meter.

One thing surprised me about this apartment: It was almost new, yet it had no hot running water. For anything except bathing, you heated water on the kitchen stove. For bathing, you flipped a switch on a water tank above the bathtub. Thirty minutes later, you had warm water. This switch actually was better than other systems. While at the Goethe Institut, Libby lived with a family where the water tank had a tray beneath it. Libby would fill the tray with coal, light it, and wait an hour until the water had warmed up from ice cold to simply cold. Then, she would step into the tub singing "A Mighty Fortress is Our God."

Rosemary and I became friends and I discovered that she had a zany sense of humor. I never knew what she was going to say or do. Neither of us had much money, but every once in awhile she would say, "I'm so rich, I wake up screaming at night!" She is the only woman I've ever met who hitchhiked through Saudi Arabia—alone.

The third person in the Munich apartment was a German woman whom I rarely saw. I can't recall her name. She just quietly shared the kitchen and bathroom with Rosemary and me. The three of us also shared something else: a headache I'll call Frau Fisch—the landlady.

When I moved in, Frau Fisch said this room was *only* for me. If I brought in anyone else to live with me, she would kick me out. She may have been worried that I would sneak 32 relatives and friends into my room. There we would live squashed together like a rock concert crowd. Of course, I would never do that. I would, however, sneak Libby in.

Libby didn't have an aunt with a Munich contact. She still was looking for a job and an apartment. Of course I wanted her to live with me until she found something. But Rosemary said the landlady often stopped by without any warning. What could we do?

One option for dealing with Frau Fisch: Pretend that Libby was "just visiting". That meant hiding her sleeping bag and luggage in my closet at the start of each day. It also meant getting dressed really early because people don't wear pajamas when they visit someone. However, to be on the safe side, Libby decided that when anyone rang the doorbell, she would leap into my closet. Hiding became Plan A. "Visiting" was Plan B.

My room had French doors that opened onto a small balcony. Frau Fisch loved fresh air. Each time she stopped by, she would throw open those French doors and say, "We must have *air!*" Not me, boy. My top priority was heat. I already had plenty of air. But I couldn't get this woman to leave the doors alone. She would fling them open with gusto. Out would go the heat from my feeble heater. In would come a blast of winter air.

Challenging authority in Germany

Frau Fisch cleaned our apartment on a regular basis and I happened to be in the kitchen one day as she cleaned the stainless steel sink. It made me wince to see her vigorously scrubbing it with an abrasive cleanser. "This woman doesn't know how to clean stainless steel," I muttered. "She's wrecking our sink." I kept this thought to myself until a week later when Frau Fisch called the three of us housemates into the kitchen, pointed to the damaged sink, and accused us of scratching it. "Excuse me, Frau Fisch," I said in my most polite tone of voice. "But I think your cleanser is causing these scratches."

Did our landlady welcome this useful piece of information? She did not. Instead, she got red in the face and began to yell. How dare I accuse her of such a thing. If she wanted to, she could throw me out on the street—right *now*. She said other things that my level of German wasn't proficient enough to understand. I did, however, catch the drift of her message: She was furious with me for challenging her authority.

Frau Fisch stomped out of the apartment after her tirade, leaving the three of us in the now-silent kitchen. After a few moments, Rosemary shrugged and said, "She's an old cow." Our German housemate gasped. "No, no", she exclaimed. "You must never say such a thing!" I turned to her in amazement. The landlady was gone. We were alone. Why not say what we were feeling? But apparently, for at least this young woman it was taboo to say anything negative about an authority figure—even in the privacy of one's own home. This was one of those moments when I felt like a stranger in a foreign culture.

Libby's job hunt

It didn't take long for Libby to tire of being dressed by 7:00 a.m. every day and hiding her belongings. Leaping into my closet became tiresome too. Each day she hunted for work and searched for housing. No luck. Finally she heard that the U.S. Army base near Munich was hiring civilians. She applied, even though she didn't want to. Why? Because the base was a separate American community—a cultural island. Libby wanted to experience Germany by working with Germans. This turned out to not be possible.

Libby may not have been thrilled to arrive at the army base, but they were thrilled to see her. She had a college degree in English She could write, type, spell, speak correct English, and fit into almost any job. It took about three minutes for the interviewer to hire her to do office work. This was their lucky day, and a lucky day for Libby as well because housing came with her job. She had a tiny attic room with a bed, a dresser, and a closet. That was better than a sleeping bag on my floor, no dresser, and a closet that was used for hiding instead of clothing.

Challenging Authority in America

While challenging authority in Germany in the 1960's was shocking, the United States was experiencing an opposite kind of shock-wave. College campuses were roiling in protests against the Vietnam War. Draft cards were burning. Betty Friedan's *The Feminine Mystique* had launched a feminist movement for women's equality. Bras were burning. And Martin Luther King's non-violent civil rights movement was morphing into a Black Power movement that said racism had to be vanquished through force. Inner cities were burning.

To someone like me, who believed in primarily using words to challenge authority, news of this violence made me wonder if I would also feel like a stranger in a foreign culture when I returned to America.

Getting hired by the U.S. Army meant that Libby and I had separate jobs and separate homes. We had been together for almost five months. We had started calling each other "my other self". It wouldn't be easy to stay in touch because the army base was outside Munich and Libby had neither a car nor a phone. If I wanted to see her, I had to drive out there, toss pebbles at her window, and hope she was home.

German fun

Rosemary had met Libby at our apartment. Now what once had been a duet became a trio in evenings and weekends. One thing we noticed about Munich in the winter: no tour buses; no camera-toting tourists. Wherever we went, we often were the only non-natives, doing the sorts of things Germans were doing for fun.

We went to beer halls, drank beer, and listened to bands play oom-pah-pah music while people sang along. We sang too. We also skied a few times at nearby ski areas. Plus, this was the season for Mardi Gras (called "Fasching" in Germany) and costume parties took place almost every night. The three of us went to several parties and stared open-mouthed at the costumes. I remember a stunning woman wearing a dress made entirely of zippers. What an outfit. And what a crowd of men standing around her, gazing at all those zippers.

Beneath all this fun, however, I could sense an unspoken past, namely, what occurred in Germany before and during World War II. One day I decided to look at that past. What I saw still haunts me.

Thoughts:

"The real voyage of discovery consists not in seeking new landscapes but in having new eyes."

Marcel Proust

Pages from my mother's 1934 diary when
she and Nanna were traveling in Germany.
(See appendix for text excerpts.)

Chapter 7:
Searching for Understanding
of an Evil Past

"Our ancestors, who sinned, are no more;
but we bear their guilt."

Book of Lamentations 5:7

Throughout my time in Germany, I kept having occasional odd encounters with strangers. Someone would come up to me and say, "I didn't know." Then he would turn and walk away. Huh? What was that? Finally I asked Margot and Ingemi what these people were talking about. "They're saying they didn't know that Jews were dying during Hitler's time," Margot said. She was 28 when "der Fuhrer"came into power in 1933, so she had vivid memories of the Nazi era and its crimes. As for the claim that someone didn't know Jews were being exterminated back then, Margot had a two-word response: "Everyone knew."

What struck me most about this topic was how nobody—young or old—talked about it. For instance, at the Goethe Institut I learned hundreds of common German words—except one. One day I naively asked a group of young teachers what the word for leader was. "Fuhrer," they said. "Oh," I replied. If such a thing as a group-blush is possible, we had one at that moment. I had just stepped into forbidden territory. I said no more, and neither did they.

I had arrived in Germany thinking that during my stay I would come to understand how, less than 30 years earlier, an entire nation could have handed over its life and its soul to a madman. Perhaps my expectation can be explained by my age: I was only 24. Furthermore,

I had never had a glimpse of what took place during Hitler's Third Reich. I had never seen a concentration camp. One day I decided to visit one: Dachau.

Dachau Concentration Camp[7]

Dachau Concentration Camp is now a memorial with exhibits for school groups, families, tourists, and scholars. It includes a monument with the words, "Lest we forget." None of that was there in 1966. Instead, what I saw looked like an abandoned site with some surviving landmarks. A sign over the entrance promised, "Arbeit Macht Frei" ("Work will make you free."). Barracks laid out in two long rows looked like storage units, except these units had once been jammed with people instead of things. And there were ovens, not for baking but for getting rid of bodies.[8]

I remember wandering around in the nearly deserted camp. The day was sunny but the place felt dark. I sensed the suffering of those who had been there. I sensed an evil that seemed to have cursed the ground itself. My brain shut down and so did my stomach. It took days for the nausea and mental numbness to wear off.

Understanding? Not possible for me then and not possible for me now. Awareness of what occurred during Hitler's Third Reich still confounds me. All I know is, I need to recognize and oppose evil whenever and wherever I encounter it. Easy to say, hard to do.[9]

---

7   For some details about the history of this concentration camp, see the appendix.

8   Dachau was set up as a work camp, not a death camp like Auschwitz. No exterminations took place there, but the death toll from disease and starvation was extremely high; ovens were used to cremate people's remains.

9   For a first-hand account of concentration camp life and death, I recommend *Night* by Elie Wiesel. For an enlightening book about the early days of the Nazi movement, I recommend *In the Garden of Beasts* by Erik Larson.

Thoughts:

"The line separating good and evil passes not through states,
nor between political parties either—but
right through every human heart."

Alexsandr Solzhenitsyn
in
The Gulag Archipelago

Chapter 8:
Encountering Working Life
—and Life Without Work

"Stand up. Keep you back straight.
Remember that this is where the wings grow."

Martha Graham, dance choreographer

I never thought I would be a permanent immigrant. But how long was I going to stay in Germany? I didn't know. A lot depended on jobs, both present and future.

Getting to work

My workplace was in downtown Munich, and I used a streetcar to get there. Unfortunately, streetcars overflowed with commuters. When a door opened, I would see people standing on the stairs in the entrance, almost falling out onto the street. But I had grown up in New York City, home of packed subways. I knew there's always room for at least *one* more rider. So in Munich I did the rude thing that others were doing: I would run at an open streetcar door and plow into the crowd standing on the bottom step. They would squeeze in just a bit. Then the door would close behind me, scraping past my clothing.

Two surprises

Working in the medical office gave me two unhappy surprises: First, the paycheck. I expected a certain salary, and I expected some deductions from that salary. But my first paycheck shocked me: Deductions added up to half of my earnings. What started out as a small salary ended up being a pitiful paycheck. It wasn't a living wage.

What surprised me most was the deduction for religion. My job application had asked about my religion. I said I was Catholic. Two weeks later, paycheck in hand, I saw that 10% of my salary had been withheld for the Catholic Church. Whatever religion you were in Germany, that church received support from the government via people's salaries.[10]

A second surprise in my job involved treatments I gave to patients. Rosemary and her boss gave patients medical care tailored to their needs. But after that, everyone went through a regime of identical treatments on a series of machines. It made no difference if you had a hand injury, or back pain, or a sprained ankle. You were put through the same paces, the same machines. I never asked anyone the reason for this, and nobody ever told me. I just quietly did what I was told to do because I needed this job.

I could see that several treatments had no value. I felt bad when I would hook up a patient to a machine that wouldn't help him. But I told myself that at least it wouldn't hurt him.

A decision

One of the machines in the office gave deep heat to patients' muscles. One day a man came in who had poor circulation in his legs. From my training in America, I knew that deep heat to that area could burn his muscles badly. Now I faced a decision: Should I do what I was told, even if it might cause harm? After six months in Germany, I knew that any questioning of a person in authority wasn't just frowned on—it was shocking and likely to lead to a cascade of disapproval. I would be risking my job if I spoke up. But I would be risking burning a patient if I said nothing.

---

10   A side note: On her job application Rosemary said she had no religion. Nevertheless, her paycheck also showed a 10% deduction for religion. We never found out who received that money.

Care for my patient won out over fear for my job, and I did what I would do in the United States in a similar situation: I talked to my boss privately and told him my concerns. As soon as I said what I was worried about, my boss began to shout at me. I backed away until I was pressed up against a wall. He kept moving forward and shouting close to my face. How dare I challenge his treatment! Then he fired me.

No more work. No more income. I had become jobless.

Life without work

Getting fired felt terrible. My head told me it wasn't my fault, but my heart told me I had done something wrong.

Another thing that felt terrible: being jobless. I was so depressed that I didn't even look for a new job. Why bother? Low language skills would keep me from working as a physical therapist, and I didn't know where to look for non-medical work. Plus, I knew the physician would never, ever give me a good recommendation.

Libby and Rosemary had jobs. Everybody in Munich seemed to have jobs. They hurried along as if they had places to go, things to do. On weekdays I was alone with no place to go and nothing to do. I sat around for a couple of weeks but then had to face a problem I couldn't ignore: Money was going out and nothing was coming in. Soon I would be broke.

Another decision

What happened next seemed to come to me out of thin air. I sat up in bed one morning knowing what I was going to do, when I was going to do it, and where I was going to work. I said, "The adventure is over. It's time for me to go home—now. I'm going to get a physical therapy job at the children's hospital in Seattle."

This last statement surprised me. I wasn't even sure where that hospital was. Plus, why did I think a job would be available when I got there? And why did I think I would be hired for that job? I had no answers to these questions. I only knew my goal. As I soon learned, achieving that goal wasn't quick and wasn't easy. Home was far away.

Thoughts:

"We must be willing to get rid of the life we've planned so as to have the life that is waiting for us."

Joseph Campbell

Chapter 9:
Not Seeking—
But Nevertheless Finding—
New Challenges

"You can't be brave if you've only had wonderful things happen to you."

Mary Tyler Moore

My adventures with Libby were over, but my journey certainly wasn't. Many miles lay between where I was in Munich and where I wanted to be in Seattle. Time to pack my bags, bid farewell to everyone and get on the road—and on the ocean.

Many goodbyes

Saying good-bye to Libby was tough because it marked the end of the adventures we had shared. Then came saying good-bye to Ingemi, also hard because I didn't know if we'd ever see each other again. And would I ever return to Germany? Leaving there meant saying good-bye to a country, a language, and a culture.

My mileage countdown to home began as I pulled out of Munich: 0 miles down, 7,000 to go. From Munich I drove to Amsterdam, a city of cyclists. Surrounded by two-wheeled vehicles, my four-wheeled vehicle looked like an intruder in a bike race. Miraculously, I arrived at the port of Amsterdam without squashing a single cyclist. There I got ready for another farewell: farewell to my trusty car for awhile. Schnapsy was going to New York City on a freighter. That would take two weeks longer than my sailing there on a passenger ship. What could I do in the interim? I decided to visit Great Britain and then catch a ship from there to New York.

After filling out mountains of forms at the port, I left most of my things in the car and walked away with a suitcase. What a difference between car versus public transportation. I was used to going wherever I wanted, whenever I wanted. Now I had to adapt to schedules and buy tickets and work out pesky details. And of course I had to travel light.

Challenges

Six months in Europe, may have made me seem like a seasoned traveler, skilled in the ways of seeing the world. Not so. Every country brought me face-to-face with a new currency, a new culture, new foods, new ways of getting around. Each time I crossed a border, I became a wide-eyed foreigner facing the unknown. Every country presented new challenges, even in Great Britain where I could again speak English.

My first challenge there came as soon as I arrived in London: I almost got killed. While waiting at a curb, I looked left see if any cars were coming. Big mistake. I forgot that in Great Britain, vehicles come from the right. As I stepped off the curb, I heard brakes screeching. Whipping around to my right, I saw that I was eyeball-to-eyeball with the headlights of a double-decker bus. I had come within inches of being plastered like a bug on the front of a bus. Whoa.

A bus driver's alertness kept me alive and I reached a train station. Now came a second challenge: the telephone. I was traveling before the age of cordless phones, cell phones, Smart phones, Twitters, and Tweets—how primitive. All telephones were hard-wired into walls. In a public place, this meant finding a pay phone if you wanted to call someone.

I looked for one of those phones in the train station. I found five of them lined up in a row like slot machines. However, these "slot machines" never put money out; they only took it in. Your reward—if you were lucky—was reaching the person you were trying to call.

I wanted to call Rosemary's parents. They lived near London and had invited me to stay with them for a few days. So I walked up to the first phone and read the directions. Oh-oh. What did a shilling look like? What about a pence? I had never seen these coins before. How many did I need of each? Was I supposed to put money into the phone before or after I dialed? Or should I wait until I reached Rosemary's parents? So many choices....

I steeled my nerves and did what I thought the phone directions were telling me to do. No luck. I tried again. Nothing. I tried doing things in a different order. Still nothing. Time passed. Each time, I failed. And each time, my frustration grew. My feelings went from fury to tears then back to fury.

Finally I asked a stranger to dial the phone for me. He did. After a few moments he said, "Oh, this one is out of order." What? All that suffering for a phone that was out of order? The man went to the next phone. Also out of order. In fact, four out of five of those phones were broken. Only the fifth one worked, and the man dialed it for me. Thank heavens for the kindness of strangers!

I reached Rosemary's mother and she started telling me which train would take me to their town. Suddenly a recorded voice broke into our conversation: If I didn't add more coins in the next 30 seconds, the call would end. I grabbed my wallet and looked in dismay at paper money. No coins. Fortunately, Rosemary's mother finished giving me directions before the phone went dead. I slammed down the receiver, muttered some bad words, and stomped off to buy a train ticket.

I love trains. I grew up traveling on them because my father worked for a railroad. So of course his children could read train schedules. We knew about gates and track numbers. And we knew that before we got on board a train, we'd better be sure which direction it was headed—east or west, north or south.

I knew all those things. What I didn't know was the London train system. It is color-coded, with each line being a different color. For a first-time visitor like me, signs looked like tangled yarn: red, brown, yellow, green, blue, gray, pink, and more. I didn't know what color I wanted. I didn't know if I needed to transfer from one line—one color—to another. I didn't know anything, but the agent who sold me a ticket did. As he handed me my ticket, he told me to hurry because my train was leaving in ten minutes.

An expression comes to mind here: "running around like a chicken with its head cut off." For the next nine minutes I was that chicken, and the chicken was hauling a heavy suitcase. I ran up to people and threw questions at them: How can I get to this gate? What track does this train come in on? Am I standing at the right place to get the train that goes to this town?

The kindness of strangers rescued me again. People pointed me in the right direction. Several of them added words such as, "You're going to make it." I thanked them as I kept running. Finally I got on board the right train, hoisted my suitcase up into a luggage rack, and sank into a seat. The train left the station a minute later as I sat catching my breath.

Broke and lonely

After leaving Rosemary's parents, several days remained before my ship would leave for America. What could I do until then? I decided to visit the country where some of Dad's ancestors had come from: Scotland. But I would have to travel very cheaply because my wallet had become so thin, I could almost see through it. Time for creative planning.

First plan: save the cost of one night's lodging by taking an overnight train to Edinburgh. So I boarded a train in the evening and slept in my seat. But I could see that saving on one night's lodging wouldn't be enough. My money would run out before I got to the ship. If I had this problem today, I would just whip out a credit card and charge everything. But in the 1960s, credit cards were rare. I didn't have one.

No credit card meant paying for everything with cash. I carried it in the form of travelers checks, and I was down to one check. What to do, what to do.... I decided to cut back on food. So I found a bed-and-breakfast place that served big breakfasts. Each morning I ate breakfast, then nothing for the rest of the day.

I do not recommend this cost-saving method. After breakfast I would feel as stuffed as one of the fat sausages I had just eaten. By evening, I would feel weak and shaky from hunger. And by the next morning I was ready to eat the pillow in my tiny room. But there was a plus side to this experience: It showed me what it must be like to go to bed hungry each night. It gave some empathy for people who never have enough to eat.

What do I remember about Scotland? Mostly I remember it as a place where I felt lonely. I missed Libby and I missed home. I was alone in a foreign country and done with this trip.

Unfortunately, 6,200 miles still stood between Edinburgh and Seattle. So I packed my suitcase for the zillionth time and got on board a train heading south toward my ship.

More Ancestors

Like many Americans, I am a blend of nationalities. My mother figured that her children were 1/4 German (because of Nanna), 3/16 Irish, 5/32 English, 1/32 Welsh, and 3/8 Scottish. (When it came to numbers, Mom always insisted on accuracy.) The Scottish part of this mix came from my father's family, a number of whom came to America in 1858 and settled in Wisconsin.

I thought I might feel the kind of connection to Scotland and its people that I had felt in Germany. That didn't happen, probably because I knew no one there— plus, by this time my sense of adventure was gone. Scotland simply felt like one more country among many I had visited.

Heading home

After only a week in Great Britain, I knew about colored lines on train schedules, odd looking coins, and cars driving on the left: I had gotten used to these just in time to leave the country on a ship heading to America.

Boy, was I glad to see that ship. For one thing, I knew it meant food because meals were included in the price of my ticket. For another thing, I thought it probably meant letters from home. I was right. Several letters were in my cabin when I got on board. One of them was a bombshell from Bob. From clear out of the blue, he said he was breaking up with me—no reason given. What a shock! We had dated for a year in Seattle. Now all of a sudden: this. As the ship sailed out of port, I stood in my cabin feeling numb and rejected. Here was another good-bye, one from home I had not expected.

I now see this letter as a good thing, but at the time it felt like a physical blow. Closing the door on dating Bob opened the door to dating Fred, whom I would marry two years later. That happy ending lay in the future, however. For the moment, I was on a ship with no way to contact anyone I knew.

More bad news: My low-budget ticket placed me in a triplex cabin with two middle-aged women who spoke no English. I don't know what they were speaking. For some reason, this distressed me more than all the other language barriers I had encountered in Europe. Perhaps I was just tired of foreign languages and reaching out to strangers. My weariness wasn't helped by the fact that my cabin mates ignored my existence and spoke only to each other. So my isolation was complete: no communication with the outside world, no words of commiseration about Bob from friends or family, no contact with my cabin mates—just me and my feelings of bewilderment and loneliness.

Instead of the excitement, anticipation and fun of sailing to Europe, the voyage home was as dull as a morning-after-the-party mood, with or without a hangover. The eight-day voyage felt more like an eight-week one. Would this trip never end? Of course it would—but not before the ocean heightened my inner turmoil with a drama of its own.

High seas

Libby and I had gone through a hurricane when we sailed from the United States to Germany. I figured that was a once-in-a-lifetime event for me. Not so. On the way back to America, this ship, too, ran into a hurricane. It felt worse than the first one because my cabin was at the stern of the ship. During the storm, the stern and the bow of the ship acted like a seesaw: The stern would go way up while the bow was way down. Then the bow would go way up while the stern was way down.

Here is how this motion looked through my cabin window: One moment all I could see would be sky—no water. The next moment, my window would be totally under water. Up and down, up and down. I longed for the movement to stop for just a few minutes so my head could stop spinning. Unfortunately, hurricanes do not pause for people. This hurricane did not pause for me.

Crazy as it sounds now, I subconsciously thought if I stayed really, really tense, somehow this tension would keep the ship afloat. Relaxing my vigilance for even a second could spell disaster: we'd all go down to the little fishies and the big, bad sea monsters. Like a toddler who believes she's in control of life itself, I believed only my tension was holding back a Titanic replay, without the iceberg. Stay alert, save the ship! And while I was saving the ship, I also had to save myself by hanging onto fixed objects wherever I went, working my way hand-over-hand through hallways and within rooms—all this while feeling dizzy from the motion. What a miserable voyage.

Hello, America

The hurricane eventually passed, as did the miles between England and the United States. Finally the ship sailed into New York Harbor. I'll never forget the sight that greeted me upon arrival. There was the Statue of Liberty, torch held high, welcoming everyone to America—immigrants, travelers, and people like me who were returning home. For me, this statue symbolized freedom. It symbolized home. It symbolized the best of my native land. It reminded me of my ancestors and of how much I cared about this country and its people, flaws and all. It brought tears to my eyes. Hello, America, I love you.

Thoughts:

"May you be blessed in your coming in."

Book of Deuteronomy 28:6a

Part Two

America

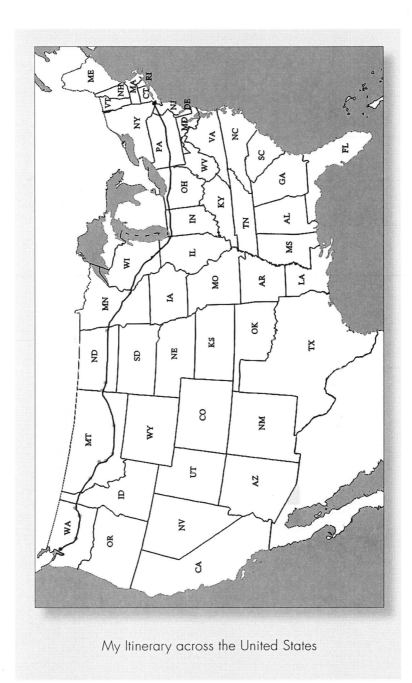

My Itinerary across the United States

Chapter 10:
Discovering America

"I have not been everywhere, but it's on my list."
Susan Sontag

Europe showed me a world I had never known: cathedrals that soared; towns that breathed history; inns that exuded charm; driving "adventures" that reinforced my belief in guardian angels; languages I had never heard; cultures I had never encountered; food I had never tasted; wine I had never drunk; and always, everywhere, unique people I had never met—and never would have met if I had stayed home in Seattle.

So I arrived in New York with memories of Europe and a broadened awareness of the world. I stepped off the ship not realizing how much I was about to discover about my own country—its beauty, its towns, its roads, its cultures, its weaknesses, its people.

Schnapsy

My mileage count to home had begun in Munich. Now 4,000 miles were behind me; 3,000 lay ahead. I would drive each of those miles in my little red car. First, however, I had to pick her up from a dock in Brooklyn. That meant subways and maps and unfamiliar streets.

By this time in my travels, I had become bold about being lost. I didn't care if people thought I was weird. Sometimes I *was* weird—like when I was going to pick up Schnapsy. I leapt on board a subway and asked in a loud voice, "Will this take me to Brooklyn?" Passengers

Childhood Memories

Contrary to what many non-natives believe, New York is more than Manhattan and skyscrapers. The city consists of five boroughs: Brooklyn, Bronx, Queens, Staten Island and, yes, Manhattan. I grew up in Douglaston, a small town on Long Island that lies within Queens Borough. Whenever we wanted to go into "the city" (alias, Manhattan), we could hop onto a Long Island Railroad train and arrive downtown in less 20 minutes.

Of course I recall Manhattan's skyscrapers, and once I went to the top of the Empire State Building—at that time the tallest building in the world. But even more vividly I remember the commuter train seats, which looked like wicker but felt like straw scratching the back of my legs and snagging my clothing.

When I was 14, our family moved to Hinsdale, Illinois, a suburb of Chicago. It was located on a Burlington Northern commuter line, and I was relieved to discover that the seats on their trains were smooth.

looked up from their newspapers, startled. But then someone said it was the wrong train. I jumped off before the doors closed, then leapt onto another train and asked the same question. Success—thanks, once again, to the kindness of strangers.

I found Schnapsy at the docks and greeted her with joy. Was she ready to drive across the United States? But first, a tougher task: Was she ready to find a parking place in New York?

New York City

My brother Dean had invited me to stay with him for a few days at his place in Manhattan, a borough with almost no parking places. Finding a legal parking spot there is a miracle. Drivers even long for illegal ones. Sometimes they settle for double parking and, hence, a slew of tickets. I don't know how parking tickets are handled now. Back then, drivers tended to ignore them. Glove compartments in many cars overflowed with unpaid tickets.

I managed to drive from the docks in Brooklyn to Dean's home in Manhattan. Then came a semi-miracle: an illegal parking place right in front of his building. Oh, happy day! I parked Schnapsy and left her there for the rest of my time in New York.

Sightseeing

Since I was in New York, why not see a couple of sights before heading West? I decided to catch a subway to Lower Manhattan and visit what in my mind was the financial center of the world: Wall Street. I expected to see important brokers rushing around. I envisioned stressed-out traders buying and selling stocks and bonds. I imagined power.

However, I visited Wall Street on a Sunday. There it was: deserted, silent, and closed. That was fine with me because it was a lovely April afternoon. If buildings could have feelings, these skyscrapers looked like they were enjoying a day of rest. They shone in the sunlight.

One structure in Wall Street surprised me: Federal Hall, on whose balcony George Washington was sworn in as first president of the United States. As I stood on the same spot where thousands had stood in 1789, I reflected on the fact that here I was, an American benefitting from something that had occurred 177 years ago. What a gift.

On the road again

Time to get on the road. I hugged Dean good-bye as he left for work then began to load my car. So much stuff, so little space. As I started loading, a taxi screeched to a halt next to me.

"Are you leaving?" the taxi driver asked.

"Not for about 20 minutes," I said.

"That's OK," he said. "I'll wait." He smiled, sat back and started to whistle. Apparently this was his lucky day: an illegal parking place—and he had to wait only 20 minutes for it.

One last task before taking off: strap my German-made skis onto a rack on the back of the car. Now I was ready. I got into Schnapsy, pulled out some maps and drove away, leaving one happy cab driver in my parking place. At the first stoplight, a guy in a sports car saw my skis and rolled down his window. "Where's the skiing?" he asked with great excitement.

"Washington State," I replied. He stared at me, looking as if he had just seen the ultimate ski nut—someone who was willing to drive 3,000 miles to find some snow. I laughed.

You're getting sle-e-e-e-py....

I left New York on a glorious morning, ready for whatever America would offer me. What I wasn't ready for was an undiagnosed condition called "central nervous system hypersomnia"—a super-sized sleepiness condition I inherited from Dad[11].

---

11 Central nervous sytem hypersomnia differs from another sleep disorder called narcolepsy. The latter is a type of seizure that strikes suddenly, whereas an attack of the former can be fought off for awhile—but not forever.

In Europe, Libby drove whenever I got sleepy. No problem. Now I was a soloist driving across a continent. Big problem.

A typical day: I get behind the wheel of the car in the morning after a good night's sleep, alert and perky and ready to drive. After about 30 minutes, an aching type of tiredness begins in my eyes. I deal with it by blinking a lot. 15 minutes pass, and I start to yawn. The yawns get bigger until I'm in danger of dislocating my jaw. In Europe, this is the point where Libby and I would switch drivers, but here I'm alone so I keep going.

Now the yawning makes my eyes water. Tears are running down my face. Brain cells urge me to take just a little nap, but my willpower fights back. "No way, you idiot!" I tell my brain. "I'm driving. This is no time for sleep."

The argument between neurons and willpower continues in a duet of weirdness. I try every technique I can think of to tip the balance in favor of willpower. Caffeine? Of course, but it only revs up my heart to 4,000 rpm's without touching my sleep center. Finally, in desperation I roll down my window, turn up the radio, slap myself silly, and sing loudly.

What I'm feeling by this point is what I can only describe as brain pain—not a headache or a stabbing sensation, but brain pain nonetheless. Neurons fire more and more powerfully, and resisting their siren call is physically painful. The brain always wins in the end, of course, and I have to pull off the road and take a nap.

And that's how my trip across America would proceed. From New York City to Seattle, I would drive for 50 or 60 minutes, then nap for 10; drive for another 50 or 60 minutes, nap for 10. Drive, nap, drive, nap. Progress was slow.

The hypersomnia wasn't overwhelming between New York and Chicago, in part because of toll booths along the way. Stopping even

"I Want to Sleep ..."

My hypersomnia was finally diagnosed in 1996 and I received medication for it. The doctor who treated me said, "You're not going to know how strange your reality has been until you're not fighting to stay awake." He was right. Blessed relief! To thank him, I wrote the following song:

I Want to Sleep All Night (and Day)

To the tune of "I Could Have Danced All Night"
from My Fair Lady

I want to sleep all night, I want to sleep all day,
And still I'll beg for more.

I want to go to bed, and rest my sleepy head;
Please tell me if I snore.

I need to know, why I am so exhausted,
Why all at once, I can't stay awake.

Is there a pill or three, that you can give to me
So I won't sleep, sleep, sleep all day?

You're tired out, dear. It's time to take a nap.

momentarily tended to revive me for awhile. Plus, the highway system in the East includes frequent gas station and restaurant combinations built over tollways like a bridge. Drivers access them for food, gas and, in my case, sleep. I believe I accessed every one of them before I pulled up to my parents' home in Hinsdale.

Family ties

I once read an anecdote by a psychiatrist who invited a colleague to join him in a visit to his parents' home. "Notice how many minutes it takes before I revert to being a child," he said to his friend. Answer: 15 minutes.

So, too, with me when I arrived in Hinsdale. In Europe, together with Libby I had managed to drive, study, work, sleep, eat, drink, be merry, get lost, find my way, and survive crises. In Hinsdale I regressed to dancing the dance of kid-dom with my folks, doing dependent things like sleeping long hours and expecting Mom do all the laundry and cooking. Meanwhile, she and Dad worried about how I could possibly make it from Hinsdale to Seattle without their assistance. Mom fussed about maps and food. (Did I have enough?) Dad fussed about my German license plates and urged me to replace them with temporary U.S. plates.

"After all," he pointed out. "What will you say if a policeman stops you on the way?"

I thought about that for a moment. "I don't know what I'll say, Dad, but you can bet I'll say it in German!"[12]

Time to go. Mom loaded me up with food and beverages. She also gave me several family items such as a footstool that Nanna had covered in needlepoint. Then came a challenge: fitting everything into my car. "Everything" included what I had taken with me to Germany, plus what

---

12   I forgot about this conversation, but Dad thought it was so funny that he submitted it to Reader's Digest. They published it in their April 1967 "Life in these United States" column.

I had gotten over there, plus things from Hinsdale.

By the time I was done, Schnapsy was as stuffed as a turkey. I told my folks they needn't worry about my getting a speeding ticket. Weighed down like this, there was no way this car could go fast enough to break any speed limits.

More family ties: Nanna

Most of my extended family lived in Madison, Wisconsin, so I routed the next leg of my trip through there. I especially wanted to see Nanna, now 87-years-old and living in a nursing home. I thought she would want to hear about Ingemi and Margot because she and Margot had corresponded for years and it was she, years earlier, who had suggested that Ingemi and I become pen pals. But to my dismay, I discovered that my grandmother had become listless and uninterested in life. She sat alone in her room, slumped over in a chair, doing... nothing.

What had happened to the Nanna I once knew? I remembered a determined, Germanic woman briskly walking up to the capital square every day to have lunch at Barons Restaurant. I, a teenager, could hardly keep up with her. I remembered a matriarch presiding over family celebrations at the Madison Club. Who was this person in front of me?

Nanna's body and brain were still present—albeit in weakened states—but her spirit was gone. Chat about Margot and Ingemi? Not interested. Talk about loved ones in Madison? No. Walk across the street to the new site of the Dean Clinic—the clinic her husband had started 60 years ago? She didn't even want to do that. I poured out loving energy, an energy that either fell at my feet or else got deflected by the shroud of depression that held my grandmother prisoner. I couldn't reach her with my love. What a helpless feeling. When I kissed her goodbye, she hardly seemed to notice.

"United States"

After my sad goodbye to Nanna, I left Madison and headed north into Minnesota. So far I had driven through eight states, and it struck me that in Europe, each of them probably would have been its own country. That would have meant stopping at every border, waiting in line, showing my passport, getting it stamped, then waiting for guards to give me permission to enter their country. Once beyond the border, I would face a new language, a new currency, and new customs—constant challenges, constant foreignness.

Now, however, the name "United States" took on new meaning. Usually the only way I could tell I was entering a new state was from two signs. First would come a sign saying "Leaving ...." A short distance later would come one saying "Entering...." What freedom.

And what a vastness I sensed in this nation. After Minneapolis, I realized the next major city would be..... Seattle. Incredible. 1,600 miles of open space. Small towns and a few medium-size cities lay along the route, but no big cities.

I have especially vivid memories of my drive through North Dakota—a state that made me wonder if this part of America had been discovered yet. I would drive for miles and see no vehicles coming towards me or going in my direction. I would see no houses, no farms, no towns. What a difference from Germany which overflowed with people. The contrast between there and here was so sharp that it felt unnerving. 13

So. No population and then also, a barren, treeless landscape. A

---

13 North Dakota underwent a radical change when energy companies developed frack-
ing to extract oil and gas from the land. A visit to the state in 2012 shocked me with
its contrast to the one I saw in 1966: drilling rigs, oil wells, monster trucks, grime,
burly wildcatters living in "man camps" of temporary shelter, and even traffic jams.
Plus, no lodging for travelers. We drove half way across the state before finding a lone
motel room in Bismarck.

thought arose as I drove: If someone parachuted a few German citizens into North Dakota, they might think they had landed on the moon. Did anyone live here? Or did this highway just arise from nothing?

Job offers

At the end of each day on my coast-to-coast drive, I would find a no-frills motel, eat at a no-frills restaurant, then phone Mom and Dad to tell them I was OK and let them know where I was staying that night.

On the night I stayed in North Dakota, the phone rang after I had called home. It was a doctor I had worked for in Seattle. He said he had called my parents to find out if they knew when I was returning to Seattle. He was delighted to learn I was headed there now because he was looking for a physical therapist. Would I like to return to work for him?

Amazingly, this was the second job offer I had received during my drive across America. The first one had come from the director of Nanna's nursing home. When she learned I was a graduate of the UW with a degree in physical therapy, she immediately showed me their PT department and said they had not yet hired staff for it. Would I like to work there? They needed a physical therapist.

Two job offers—even before I reached Seattle! What a contrast with Munich, where job hunting and rejections had made me wonder if anyone would notice if I slipped off the edge of the earth. Now I felt valued; memories of Munich began to fade. However, my eyes and dreams were focused on that children's hospital. Reluctantly I turned down both invitations but in each case felt a glow that comes from being wanted.

"You're getting extremely sleepy...."

The term "highway hypnosis" may have been coined by someone while driving through the flat emptiness of North Dakota and eastern

Montana. That scenery, combined with my hypersomnia, created a constant danger. It reminds me of something I recently read: "Regular naps prevent old age, especially if you take them while you're driving."

The only effective technique I had discovered for keeping awake behind the wheel was mental stimulation. Conversing in German could keep me going for hours. A lively conversation in English would have the same effect; so, too, a thought-provoking radio program. None of these opportunities existed in the western half of the United States because not only was I driving solo, often I couldn't even locate a radio station. The only signal my brain was receiving was the one telling me to sleep.

What to do, what to do.... Rest areas were scarce; even exits were rare. So when my eyelids began to sink and my consciousness fade, I would pull off onto the highway shoulder, tilt the driver's seat back, and nap. Dangerous? Definitely. But it worked, and I could imagine the alternative: fall asleep, crash, meet my Maker. I didn't want to do that just yet.

A meet-my-Maker event almost occurred in Montana when the hypersomnia overpowered my willpower and common sense. I fell asleep. There were no rumble strips back then to alert drivers to the fact that they were running off the road. People just woke up in a ditch—or sometimes never woke up. So yes, I fell asleep; but no, I didn't end up in a ditch. By some miracle, I awoke while still on the highway shoulder. Whoa! My eyes popped open as a shot of adrenal hit my brain. For the next half hour, shock kept me super-awake, heart pounding and every muscle tensed. Then, 30-minutes older and a whole lot wiser, I pulled over and took a nap.

Super slow

An hourly ten-minute nap tends to extend the length of a good ol' girl's trip. In Eastern Montana, Mother Nature added another impediment to slow me down: crosswinds. They came howling at me from out of the south, as if a giant hand were pushing against the left side of my car in order to shove me off the road. To counteract the pressure, I kept pulling on the steering wheel as if I wanted to turn left. That technique worked OK except for a single harrowing moment: a moment one morning when the highway passed between two house-sized boulders that blocked the wind.

One second I was pulling hard to the left on the steering wheel; the next second I was in the left-hand lane. How did I get there? It felt as if a strange air current had picked up my car and placed it in the other lane. I hadn't steered there—I had just landed there. And wouldn't you know? Headed towards me was a pickup truck—this, in an area where I usually saw about one vehicle per hour. I swerved back into my lane and missed the truck by inches. Just another adrenaline moment on my trek across America. I tightened my grip on the steering wheel, told my heart to quit pounding, and kept on going.

The crosswinds were merciless throughout the entire eastern half of Montana—hundreds of miles. Whenever I took a break, I could hardly straighten out my fingers. They were locked in a curled position. I hadn't encountered conditions like this while driving in Europe—or anywhere else, for that matter. It gave new meaning to the term "Wild West."

Then came the Rocky Mountains and the challenge of crossing over them in a 4-cylinder, under-powered vehicle. Schnapsy huffed and puffed her way up those passes, often at 20 miles per hour. Coming down the other side was fun. Whee! Then would come another climb. Downshift from 4th gear into 3rd; downshift from 3rd into 2nd. Go slower... and slower... and slower.... as big American cars fly by. At the top of each pass, usually a few of those big cars would be sitting at the side of the road with their radiators boiling over. I couldn't keep from smirking as my car with her little air-cooled engine kept on going.

America the beautiful

Driving throughout Europe had given me a sense of its uniqueness and beauty. My drive across the United States gave rise to similar feelings, only now I was traveling not as a foreigner but as someone who belonged here. I had lived in, worked in, and/or visited a number of areas in America. I had flown over it and ridden across it on trains. But it wasn't until I drove from one coast to the other—mile after mile after mile—that I began to grasp the vastness, the variety, and the magnificence of my own country.

The closer I got to home, the more excited I got. Here came that drowsing volcano: Mount Rainier. Hello, you gorgeous thing. Stay asleep! And here were other snow-covered peaks. Hello, you jagged things. You're gorgeous too. Now here came evergreen trees, reaching up to touch the sky. Hello, trees, you look different from ones back East. They're so round and you're so pointy.

Then finally, here came the last pass before Seattle: Snoqualmie. Schnapsy climbed it in her usual super-slow style, then zipped down into Western Washington. Now I really was almost home. Here came the suburbs, then Lake Washington. I crossed the I-90 floating bridge on a Thursday afternoon and rolled into town.

Hello, Seattle. I'm back! I have no money, I have no job, I have no place to live, but I'm back.

Thoughts:

"One cannot be an American by going around saying that one is an American. It is necessary to feel America, like America, love America and then work."

Georgia O'Keeffe

Treating 6-year-old Lisa, who had been hit by a car.

Chapter 11:
Finding New Beginnings

"There is nothing like returning to a place that remains unchanged to find ways in which you yourself have altered."

Nelson Mandela

I pulled into Seattle with $20 in my pocket, no job, and nowhere to live. For months I had been blessed by the kindness of strangers. Now came the kindness of friends: David and Betty. They were storing some things I had left with them before my trip. When I pulled up to their house, they greeted me with open arms. And when they found out I needed housing, they invited me to stay with them for a few weeks even though their home already was filled with a newborn baby and a toddler.

Working in America

I had been dreaming about Children's Hospital for 7,000 miles, two continents, and one ocean. Time to see if a job was available. So the day after I got back, I found the hospital, found the PT department, and asked the director if there was a job opening. She said one of their therapists had retired earlier that week. Would I like to replace her? Yes, I would. Could I start work on Monday? Yes, I could!

The timing of this event still amazes me. It took weeks to go from Munich to Seattle. In Germany when I said I was going to get this job, how could I have known it would be available the same week I arrived? Was it a "God thing"? I think so.

What a difference between my job in Munich and the one in Seattle. The job at Children's was at a professional level. It paid a living wage. And if I had concerns about a treatment, I felt free to discuss those concerns with a doctor or another medical person. I had no fear that I'd get fired. Instead, staff members worked together as a team.

In my earlier work in Seattle as a PT, I had treated adult outpatients. Now I was treating young inpatients. I treated children with fractures, head injuries, cerebral palsy, cystic fibrosis, third-degree burns; children who had been abused, who were dying from cancer or recovering from surgery. Together they had one thing in common: They needed healing.

I loved the patients and I loved the work, but boy, was it draining. I rejoiced when a child recovered, wept when a child died. Joy or sorrow, and sometimes both, I left work each day completely used up—fulfilled, but used up.

New shoes

When I returned to Seattle, my season as a wandering young adult ended and a new one began. For about six months, it felt like a pair of ill-fitting shoes because I had expected to pick up my life where it had left off nine months earlier. But those "shoes" of my pre-journey life no longer fit me.

I thought I would reunite with my single friends. Much to my amazement, all of them were gone. My former roommate had married and moved to Canada; another friend had moved to Pennsylvania; I had no clue where the others were. Bob was in Montana—and besides, we were no longer dating. Fred was in graduate school in Washington DC.

Then came the let-down that often occurs after a big adventure: Day-to-day life looked so... dull. In Germany, even ordinary topics weren't ordinary because I was speaking a foreign language. I had to think hard about everything I said and heard. Every conversation felt deep. Now that I was back to speaking English, dull topics were back to being dull. The weather? Boring. What to wear? Boring. Grocery choices? Boring. In short, I was depressed.

I also was distressed because I saw something I had never fully recognized when I was immersed in the American culture: its focus on materialism and money. Ads urged you to buy, buy, buy. If you did that, you would be happy, happy, happy. Not only would you be happy, you also would be popular. Lucky you. You could have it all.

It took some time, but after I had worked at Children's for awhile and after Fred returned to Seattle and we resumed dating, I started to feel like I was truly home—home in Seattle, home in America.

Closing thoughts:

It is possible to leave home but stay in a cocoon. It also is possible to leave and discover the world. My time overseas helped me discover the wider world and also America. It changed me and changed the course of my life.

Nearly fifty years have passed since I embarked on my grand adventure. Eight years after my return, I set forth on an even grander adventure—the inward one. It is this deeper journey of self-discovery and of God that has had the biggest impact on my life.[14]

_____

14   For a description of my deeper journey, see the Afterword.

I began this book with a poem called "Quest", written by my father's cousin, Elizabeth. She also wrote another poem with the same title that brings to mind this second journey:

Quest

Elizabeth Brigham Rooney

Lots of people
Go
Back and forth,
Yon and hither
To and fro.

Instead,
I'm busy learning
To be still
Here
On this low, blue hill.

Not only still,
But stilled
And open to God's will
And filled.

Daughters Beth and Kathy, age 3,
at Seattle's Woodland Park Zoo

Epilogue:
Whatever happened to....

What happened to me?

I had returned to Seattle in 1966. Fred returned in 1967, and we got married in 1968. Eighteen months later I gave birth to identical twin girls. I stayed home as a full-time parent while Fred worked at Boeing as an airlines analyst.

Our daughters are married now and I have become a writer. Fred retired in 2004 after working at Boeing for 40 years. The two of us continue to travel because we love to see the world. We also love to see our four grandchildren, who are pure joy.

What happened to Libby?

Libby returned to the United States six months after I did. We've gotten together only a few times since then, but a bond of shared experiences continues to unite us. I'm amazed at the things she remembers that I've forgotten. Her feedback while writing this book was invaluable.

Libby now is the grandmother of seven, all of them adopted from foreign orphanages: three children from Kazakhstan, two from Ethiopia, one from Vietnam, and one from Korea. I'm struck by how different their arrival in America was from that of my great-grandparents, yet they, too, are immigrants in this nation of both new and old immigrants.

What happened to Ingemi?

Ingemi married her fiancé, Claus, in 1967. She finished her studies and became a veterinarian, while Claus became a science teacher. They have a son and a daughter and now live in a German town near the Danish border.

In 2009 Ingemi and Claus drove to Prague when Fred and I were there for a few days. I had not spoken German for 43 years. Ingemi had not studied English for 46 years. Claus did not know English. Fred did not know German. Hm-m-m. Would this be a mute reunion?

Fortunately Ingemi and I had brought English/German dictionaries with us. Each of us dug into our language memory and were surprised at how much we could recall. We translated for our husbands. We used the dictionaries. We used gestures. We laughed and told stories. Today we continue to stay in touch via email and can even see each other through the wonders of the Internet. Seven thousand miles is not so far away.

What happened to Rosemary?

Rosemary left Munich six months after I did. She eventually moved to Australia where she established an osteopathic practice. Fred and I had an opportunity to visit her in Perth in 2012. I rejoice in the time we had together, wrapped in warm sunshine on her patio, reminiscing about our time in Germany. As with Libby and me, Rosemary delights in her grandchildren—twin boys.

What happened to Schnapsy?

My little red Volkswagen Beetle was such a part of my travels that she was like a person to me. Alas, her life was short: One morning in 1970 while Fred was driving to work, Schnapsy was rear-ended by a car going 40 mph. She ended up looking like an accordion, her engine only a few inches behind the driver's seat. Fred, thank God, was not injured.

In a way, the end of Schnapsy truly brought my European travels to an end. What stories. What memories. What an adventure.

One final thought:

"Every American is a traveler or a descendant of travelers."

William Least Heat Moon

Afterword:
A Different Quest

My travels in 1965 began because I sought a "grand adventure". In 1973, I began a different quest when a chronic illness reduced me to a skeletal size. I turned to God in desperation when the medical community ran out of guesses and all other options failed. I realized only God knew what was going on within my diminishing body. Words from the psalmist could have been my words as well: "Out of the depths I cry to you, O Lord. O Lord, hear my voice."

My 1973 quest was more focused than the one in 1965. Now I wanted only one thing: a cure. And it happened—28 years later. During the intervening years, the waxing and waning, sometimes maddening, sometimes inactive illness drew me into an ever-deeper relationship with the Risen Lord. Where God had once sat securely on a Sunday morning shelf, he eventually became a central focus for each day—an anchor, a consoler, a teacher, a savior.

My relationship with God continues today. I find solace and challenge in scripture, especially through the lives of those whose spiritual journeys are recorded in its pages—people such as:

Jeremiah—"You duped me, Lord, and I let myself be duped."

Moses—"If you please, Lord, send someone else!"

Mary—"My soul proclaims the greatness of the Lord."

I wrestle, resist, wonder and laugh. Many days, I simply show up because I'm committed to this relationship. It sustains me.

Ultimately my illness led to a writing career and a healing ministry within and beyond the Catholic Church. I am living proof of God's ability to bring good out of something bad. Personal prayer keeps me going, as do the church's sacraments and my relationships with countless Christians. Without them, I would be a rootless tree with no lasting strength, no ability to withstand drought or the storms of life. I thank God for these people and for the Church and for all that they have given me.

As noted at the end of Chapter 11, my inward journey has been a far grander adventure than the one I embarked on in my mid-20s. I still seek understanding but accept that I'll never completely find it in this life. I seek happiness but know that sadness will always be part of it. I seek wholeness but realize it will only fully arrive in heaven.

I pray for all of you who, like me, seek adventures and answers and wholeness and, yes, even God. May the God of surprises give you more than you expect. May you find what Jesus said God wants each us to have: fullness of life (Jn 10:10).

Come, Holy Spirit.

Jan

www.JanAlkire.com

APPENDIX

GERMANY:
A BIT OF HISTORY.

The Germany that Libby and I experienced in the 1960s was strikingly different from what it is today:

Germany at the time of our visit:

West Germany and the city of West Berlin were democratic.

East Germany (including East Berlin) was Communist and was behind what had come to be known as the Iron Curtain that separated free Western Europe from Communist Eastern Europe.

West Berlin existed in democratic isolation in the middle of Communist East Germany.

How had this confusing situation come to be? Here's a summary of what occurred during the 20 years prior to our visit:

May 1945: Nazi Germany was defeated and became occupied by a coalition of four World War II Allied forces: the United States, Great Britain, France, and the Soviet Union. The German capitol, Berlin, was also divided up and administered by these nations.

May 1949: U.S., British, and French zones merged to become *West Germany* (the Federal Republic of Germany)—a democratic country. Soviet Union maintained control over what became known as *East*

Germany (the German Democratic Republic)—not democratic at all, but Communist. The Soviet-controlled section of Berlin became *East Berlin*. The other three sectors became *West Berlin*.

Up until August 1961: East Germans (including East Berliners) were allowed to work in West Berlin and return home at night. Increasingly, workers were refusing to go back. By mid-1961, thousands per day were defecting to Western Europe through West Berlin.

August 1961: To stop the flood of East Germans escaping through West Berlin, East Germany built the *Berlin Wall* between East and West Berlin. It consisted of three elements: two parallel barriers plus a "death strip" in between. Anyone entering the death strip was shot on sight from one of the wall's many guard towers.

Dachau Concentration Camp

The Internet contains much information about Dachau. Here are a few facts:

Located about ten miles outside of Munich on the grounds of an old munitions factory.

Opened in 1933, only 51 days after Hitler came into power: the first—and longest running—Nazi concentration camp of the Third Reich.

Initially a camp for political prisoners, eventually used for everyone, including Jews.

Had a "priests block" with over 2,700 priests who opposed the Nazi regime.

Cause of death for most prisoners: starvation or disease (especially typhus). Suicides also common.

Liberated by American troops on April 29, 1945.

Barracks were designed to house 250 prisoners. At time of liberation, each held 1,600.

Camp remained in use after the end of the war—initially as a prison for camp guards and other Nazis, then later as housing for refugees and for those left homeless by the war.

Excerpts from my mother's
1933/34 diary

My mother began keeping a diary in 1933 while doing post-graduate studies in London. Nanna (Mom's mother) joined her at the end of the school year for a drive through Europe. Here are excerpts from Mom's diary, including her first impressions of Nazis.[15]

May 19, 1934: "First thing we saw on the German border was a nice young man in uniform, wearing a swastika armband. He saluted in a peculiar way. The other customs man tried to convince mother that all the stories we heard about Germany were wrong and that they were a very happy people. They seem to be, as they always sing when they're together with fine voices and harmony. Lots of marching, brownshirts, and swastikas...."

May 20: "Woke up at 5:30 by rattling of drums and marching as usual."

May 27: "I've never in all my life seen so many uniforms and so much marching as they do here. It looks ominous. Most of the marchers are young boys and girls, always carrying rucksacks."

Mom and Nanna's trip included Oberammergau, Germany, where they saw a production of the town's Passion Play about the suffering, death, and Resurrection of Jesus Christ.

The history of Oberammergau's play goes back to 1633 when the bubonic plague was decimating the town. In desperation, the villagers gathered around a cross and made a sacred vow to God: The entire town would regularly perform a Passion Play if no more people died

---

15   Chapter 7 includes a photograph of two pages from this diary.

of the plague. Their chronicles record that from that day forward, the "Black Death" claimed no more victims.

The people of Oberammergau have kept their word. Over 2,000 local people now perform the play throughout the first year of each decade. Because 1934 was its 300ᵗʰ anniversary, it was offered then as well. Mom called it a highlight of her trip. Excerpts from her diary:

May 20, 1934: "Oberammergau and it's simply grand. Staying in a nice comfortable home in this neat, interesting village. It seems so strange to see all the boys and men with long hair.... Lots of wood carving for sale and would like to buy more than we can.

"Tonight fires lit on 7 mountains around to commemorate plague fires 300 years ago when the play started. Old way to show a plague in locality."

May 21: "The Passion Play and it was marvelous. It's difficult to believe that these villagers could put on such a large and successful production. The colors, singing, mob acting, individual acting, and the tableaux were superb."

Family recipe

Here is a cookie recipe from a German maid Nanna had when Mom and her two brothers were growing up. The maid's name was Liesel, so we call these cookies Lieselkuchen (i.e., Lisa's cookies). Ingredients are in odd amounts because Liesel brought this with her from Germany, where ingredients at that time were measured in ounces.

Lieselkuchen

1 package (4 ounces) German sweet chocolate
4 ounces pecans*
3/8 C sugar (i.e., 1/4 cup + 2 T)
2½ cups sifted flour
1 teaspoon vanilla
9 ounces <u>real</u> butter (i.e., 2 sticks + 2 T)

Grind or grate together the chocolate and nuts.
(The chocolate is so hard, I use my Cuisinart, but if I get carried away, the chocolate gets too warm and melts—not good!)
Mix chocolate, nuts, sugar, flour, and vanilla.
Cut in the butter, as for pie crust.
Make small balls, set on ungreased cookie sheet.
(This step takes a bit of practice!)
Bake slowly (250 degrees) for about 40 minutes.
(Cookies look the same when they're done because there's no leavening in the batter. They start—and end—dark in color.)
Roll while warm in granulated sugar.

* According to the University of Wisconsin's Max Kade Institute (with whom I shared this recipe), pecans are probably a "new country" substitute for "old country" nuts: hazelnuts.

ACKNOWLEDGMENTS

This book would not exist without the encouragement and wisdom of those who kindly gave me feedback on its many drafts. They include Libby, Joan Bell, Candy Stickney, Pat King, and the creative folks in a North Seattle writing class.

Special thanks my husband, Fred, for his photos, and to Ray Meuse for his amazing skill in editing this book's illustrations and preparing them for publication.

I am especially indebted to my traveling friend, Libby, whose memory of our shared adventures was/is better than mine.

Finally, I am indebted to my mother, who gathered data and took the time to write down numerous bits and pieces of our family history. Where would history be without its scribes?